ON THE ROAD

the art of the journey

Published by **Pearson Education**

London • New York • San Francisco • Toronto • Sydney • Tokyo • Singapore
Hong Kong • Cape Town • Madrid • Amsterdam • Munich • Paris • Milan

REUTERS

PEARSON EDUCATION LIMITED

Edinburgh Gate
Harlow CM20 2JE
Tel: +44 (0)1279 623623
Fax: +44 (0)1279 431059
Website: www.pearsoned.co.uk

First published in Great Britain in 2005

© Reuters 2005

ISBN 0 131 29697 3

British Library Cataloguing-in-Publication Data
A catalogue record for this book is available from the British Library

Library of Congress Cataloging-in-Publication Data
A catalogue record for this book is available from the Library of Congress

10 9 8 7 6 5 4 3 2
08 07 06 05 04

Publisher: Jaime Marshall
Managing Editor: Julie Knight
Reuters editors: Simon Newman and Jassim Ahmad

With special thanks to: Louise Buckley, Alexia Singh, Angela Kearney, Wiebke Singer, Susan Allsopp, Dafydd Piercy, Heather Vickers

Designed by Maggie Wells and Andrea Bannuscher
Typeset by 30
Printed and bound in Great Britain by Bath Press

The publisher's policy is to use paper manufactured from sustainable forests.

The images in this book were taken in the course of news gathering and/or journalistic activities for or by Reuters. None of the subjects within any of the images sponsors or endorses the book in any way.

FOREWORD

Life is a journey. Every day, everybody is going somewhere. *On the Road* takes readers on a trip around the world, exploring the colour, contrasts and challenges of travel. The road we travel can lead to a physical or spiritual destination.

The journey along it can be for fun or for survival. It can represent a daily routine or the trip of a lifetime. For some the destination is never reached and being on the road becomes a way of life. The pictures in this book, produced by Reuters award winning team of photographers, provide a unique insight into these journeys. Reuters photographers are always on the road. Always there to capture the exceptional image which provides an impartial yet unique insight into people, places and cultures.

Their stunning pictures tell us much about both the wonders and challenges of everyday life around the globe. Whether it is refugees fleeing for their lives, the passion of a protest, an epic voyage, or the excitement of a local festival, a Reuters photographer will be there to capture their essence.

The commitment of Reuters journalists to getting the best possible picture is absolute, even taking pictures in dangerous situations. Their images offer us a unique and compelling insight into the many different experiences the world has to offer.

Monique Villa and Thomas Szlukovenyi

Radu Sigheti
11 December 2002

An Afghan shepherd leads his flock to Kabul.

Petr Josek
28 December 2003

A woman skates on a frozen pond near the small city of Bystrice, Czech Republic.

Patrick Price
30 December 2003

Longtime cowboy Bill Collins leads over 300 cattle from their autumn pasture to their ranch along a road northwest of Calgary during the annual cattle drive.

David Gray
31 March 2004

Two young Buddhist monks campaign opposite the Town Hall during a ceremony in central Colombo.

4

Sergio Pérez

12 March 2004

Hundreds of thousands of citizens gather around Colon Square at the start of a silent march through Madrid to mourn victims of the bombing of four packed commuter trains.

Jayanta Shaw
1 December 2003

An Indian sex worker looks out of the window of a
decorated tram used as part of an AIDS prevention
awareness campaign on World AIDS Day in Calcutta.

Kieran Doherty
7 May 2003

An Iraqi woman holds her child on board the first
passenger train to leave Baghdad bound for Basra
since the toppling of Saddam Hussein.

Hazir Reka
3 May 2004

A Kosovo Albanian child sits outside his grandfather's house, which has an old car door used as a window, in Pristina.

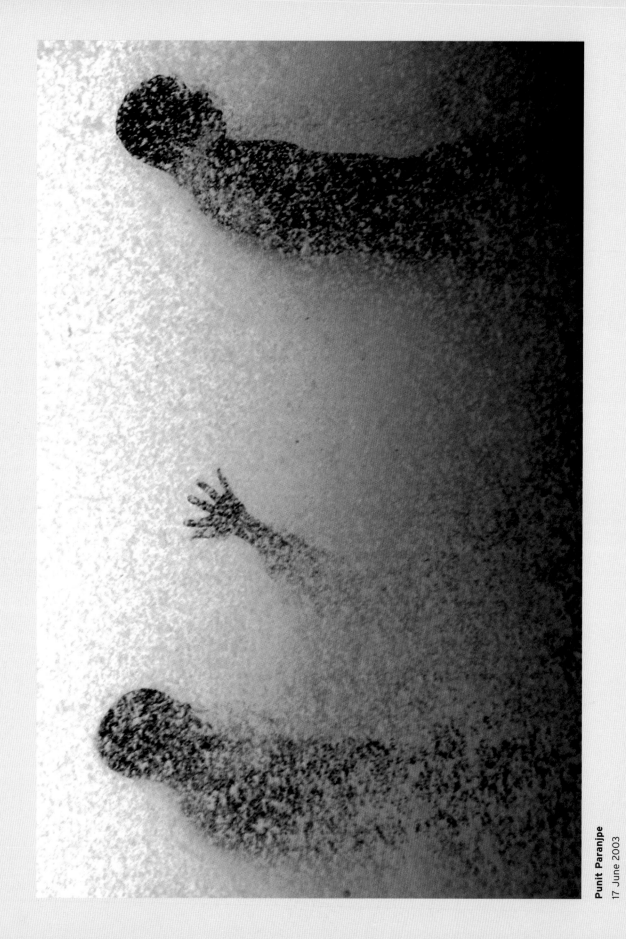

Punit Paranjpe
17 June 2003

Indian boys enjoy the splash from huge sea waves
in Bombay at the start of the Monsoon season.

Damir Sagolj

13 November 2003

A soldier of the U.S. Army's 4th Infantry Division conducts an early morning search for Iraqi militants hidden in dense vegetation around the Diala river near the northeastern Iraqi town of Baquba.

Kieran Doherty
26 June 2004

A reveller wearing wellington boots walks through
mud on a rainy day at the Glastonbury music
festival in the southern English county of Somerset.

Shamil Zhumatov

Born in Almaty, Kazakhstan, 1971

Shamil started to work for a local newspaper in 1987. He joined Reuters in 1994 covering the former Soviet Asian republics: Kazakhstan, Kyrgyztan, Tajikistan, Turkmenistan and Uzbekistan. Shamil covered events in Afghanistan including the earthquake in 1998 and the 2001-2002 war. He was also part of a team covering Iraq in 2003.

Thomas White

Born in Zambia, 1969

Thomas started work as a commercial photographer in France. In 1992 he joined a French agency and covered central Africa. Five years later he settle in Miami, doing assignments in Africa, Latin America and Europe, and continued his commercial work in fashion and advertising. In 2000 he move to Singapore and after two years at the *Straits Times* he joined Reuters.

Darren Whiteside

Born in Toronto, Canada, 1965

Darren has worked for Reuters since 1995 and is based in Phnom Penh, Cambodia. Some of the most interesting places he has worked are Somalia, Japan, Afghanistan and East Timor.

Arnd Wiegmann

Born in Berlin, Germany, 1961

Having trained as an advertising photographer, Arnd began working as a photographer in 1990 and began freelancing for Reuters in 1993.

Tim Wimborne

Born in Melbourne, Australia, 1969

Tim has been working as a photographer since 1993. He worked as a freelancer in a dozen countries shooting stills for television networks and magazines. He began freelancing for Reuters in Sydney in 2001, spent a yea doing the same in San Francisco and returned to Sydney to take up a staff position in 2003.

Andrew Wong

Born in 1962

Andrew Wong has been working for Reuters since the inception of Reuters News Pictures. He has worked in Hong Kong, London, Singapore and Beijing for the last 20 years. Andrew covered major stories in Africa, Asia and Europ

Bobby Yip

Born in Hong Kong, 1962

Bobby started work as a local newspaper and magazine photographer before joining Reuters in 1990 as a photographer and sub-editor. In 1997 he became photographer for the Hong Kong bureau. Bobby was the chairman of the Hon Kong Press Photographers Association in 1994, 1999, 2003 and 2004.

Remy Steinegger
Born in Locarno, Switzerland, 1957

Remy became a photographer in 1984 after training as a teacher. He began working for Bild & News and then for the Associated Press in Switzerland before joining Reuters in 1992 as a freelance photographer reporting mostly from southern Switzerland.

Juan Carlos Ulate
Born in Costa Rica, 1962

Juan Carlos started working as a photographer for Costa Rica's *La Republica* newspaper. He won Costa Rica's National Journalism Award for photos he took while injured in a terrorist bombing in 1984. He joined Reuters in 1990 and has covered many events including Pope John Paul's visits to Nicaragua and Guatemala, and Presidential and WTO summits in Mexico.

Miguel Vidal
Born in Pontevedra, Spain, 1968

Miguel began photography by chance in 1992 and in 1994 started work with a local newspaper. He joined Reuters in 1999, and has covered stories in Cuba, Kosovo and London.

Paul Vreeker
Born in the Netherlands

Paul started as a junior photographer with a local newspaper at the age of sixteen. He has worked for several publications, provided photography for advertising campaigns and worked for ANP, the Dutch national press agency. Paul started with Reuters in 2001. During his career he has covered events such as the Summer and Winter Olympics and state visits with the Dutch royal family.

Vincent West
Born in Southampton, United Kingdom, 1966

After studying Anthropology at London University, Vincent worked as a boat builder, sailor and freelance photographer, collaborating with various specialist magazines and the *Independent* newspaper. He has worked for Reuters in the Basque Country for eight years.

Paulo Whitaker
Born in São Paulo, Brazil, 1960

Paulo began working as a staff photographer in 1987, on the biggest Brazilian Newspaper, "*Folha de Sao Paulo*". He then worked for Agence France-Presse in São Paulo. He joined Reuters in 1997 and is based in São Paulo.

Mohammed Salem
Born in Gaza, 1985

Mohammed joined Reuters in 2001 and has covered news and clashes between Palestinians and Israelis in the Gaza Strip.

Suhaib Salem
Born in Gaza, 1979

After working one year as a cameraman with Gulf TV, Suhaib joined Reuters in 1997. He has covered major news stories in Iraq, Saudi Arabia, Jordan, Iran, the United Arab Emirates, and the 2002 World Cup in Japan and South Korea. He has won several awards including the 2001 World Press Photo prize and was named Reuters Photographer of the Year in 2002.

Jayanta Shaw
Born in Calcutta, India, 1966

Jayanta started his career in 1986 as a freelance photographer in Calcutta. He then joined the Bengali daily *Bartaman* before joining Reuters in 1988. Since then he has covered many news events in India and is based in Calcutta. Jayanta was awarded 2nd prize in the print category of the Nikon International Photo contest in 2003.

Radu Sigheti
Born in Bucharest, Romania, 1959

Radu started work in the photo studio of Romania's biggest printing house in 1980. He later joined *Romania*, a monthly magazine published for embassies abroad and has been working for Reuters since October 1990.

Jorge Silva
Born in Mexico City, Mexico, 1975

Jorge Silva began working with Agence France-Presse in 1998 in Mexico. He joined Reuters in 2000 as a freelance photographer based in Guatemala City. He became a full-time staff photographer in 2003 when he moved to Venezuela, based in Caracas. He has covered news stories in Latin America and the Caribbean region.

Shannon Stapleton
Born in Fort Bening, USA, 1968

Shannon has worked for Reuters since 2000 and has covered the Kosovo crisis, Sierra Leone and other news assignments.

Hazir Reka
Born in Ferizai, Kosovo, 1961

Hazir began working as a professional photojournalist in 1984 before joining Reuters in 1998. He has covered war and protests in Kosovo, followed the NATO-led peacekeeping force KFOR in the Balkan region and covered assignments in Iraq. He was named Photographer of the Year in 2003 by the Kosovo Association of Professional Journalists.

Stefano Rellandini
Born in Milan, Italy, 1963

Stefano started work at a Milan photographic still studio, and moved from there to the sports agency Pentaphoto. He has covered a range of events including the Summer and Winter Olympics, the Skiing World Cup, tennis and fashion. Since he started work as a freelance photographer for Reuters in the mid 1990s, he has covered events such as the Giro d'Italia and the death of Versace.

Max Rossi
Born in Rome, Italy, 1965

Max began freelancing for national newspapers and magazines in 1991. From 1996 to 2002 he worked exclusively for *Famiglia Cristiana* magazine covering national and international stories. In 2003 Max joined Reuters as a freelance photographer.

Pascal Rossignol
Born in Lille, France

Pascal started photo assignments in 1981 with newspapers in northern France. He began working for Reuters in 1985. Based in Lille, Pascal is also a volunteer fireman, and regularly shoots pictures for French emergency services. He instructs journalism at the University of Lille and is also a keen underwater photographer.

Damir Sagolj
Born in Sarajevo, Bosnia, 1971

Having been in the Bosnian army for five years and worked for the Paris-based Sipa press agency as their Bosnian photographer, Damir joined Reuters in 1997. Based in Sarajevo, Damir has covered events in the Balkans, Middle East and Americas from major news to sports events. His work has been published in leading magazines and newspapers worldwide.

Akram Saleh
Born in Iraq, 1973

Akram started work as a photographer when he was 12 years old in his father's studio. His news career started with several local newspapers, such as *al-Qadisiya* and the Iraqi News Agency. Having freelanced for Reuters for events such as the 1988 bombing campaign, Akram started working for Reuters exclusively in 2002. His awards include first prize in Baghdad's International Fair (2000-2001)

Punit Paranjpe

Born in Bombay, India, 1977

Punit began working as a freelance photographer at the age of nineteen. He
joined *Outlook*, a leading Indian news weekly, in 1999 and covered major
breaking news stories all over India. Several of his pictures made it to the
cover of the magazine. He started working for Reuters from January 2003 as
a freelance photographer.

Sergio Pérez

Born in Madrid, Spain, 1972

Sergio joined Reuters in 1991 as a freelance photographer, becoming staff in
1996. During this time he has covered all kinds of events around the world such
as the Sydney Olympics, Japan/Korea World Cup and Euro 2004 in Portugal.
He also covers many political, entertainment, sporting and diplomatic events
inside and outside his country working both as a photographer and as an editor.

Patrick Price

Born in Kingston, Ontario, 1957

Patrick has been shooting for Reuters since the company first began
operations in Canada in 1985. Having started working on oil rigs he re-trained
as a photographer and has previously freelanced for several newspapers and
the United Press Canada wire service.

José Luis Quintana

Born in Jauja, Peru, 1960

José Luis worked as photographer for *Cambio* magazine in Peru and various
newspapers in Bolivia. He joined Reuters as a freelance photographer in
October 2003 during Bolivia's political crisis.

Rafiqur Rahman

Born in Dhaka, Bangladesh, 1950

Rafiqur started his career as a press photographer in 1970, working with local
newspapers. In 1982, he began working as a camera operator with Reuters
Television and in 1986 he started taking still pictures for the Reuters News
Pictures service. Rafiqur continues to be based in Dhaka.

Jason Reed

Born in Sydney, Australia, 1970

Jason joined Reuters in Sydney in 1990 as a news pictures assistant, while
studying a technical degree in photography. Jason spent nine years covering
news, sports and feature stories across Asia for Reuters. In early 2003, he
moved to Washington D.C., where he now works as a Senior Photographer,
covering the White House and other U.S. stories.

Jeff joined Reuters in 1996, based in Scotland. He has covered a variety of events including the funerals of the Queen Mother and Princess of Wales, the wedding of pop star Madonna, the 1998 World Cup Finals in France and the Salt Lake City Winter Olympics. Jeff has won numerous awards.

Peter Morgan
Born in New Hampshire, USA, 1955

Peter started working as a freelance photographer for the Associated Press after graduating from Boston University in 1979. After working in the north-eastern U.S. and Central America, he joined Reuters as a freelance photographer in New York in 1992 and was hired as a Senior Photographer in 1998.

Bazuki Muhammad
Born in Kuala Lumpur, Malaysia, 1965

Bazuki graduated with a Bachelor of Architecture degree from Louisiana State University in the United States. He has photographed American sports since he was 17. In 1998, he joined Reuters, based in Kuala Lumpur. He covers politics, features, sports and economic news stories.

Aladin Abdel Naby
Born in Cairo, Egypt, 1955

Aladin became a photographer in 1981. He joined Reuters in 1986 after being commissioned to cover the World Squash Championships in 1985. Aladin has covered events in North and Central Africa, the Middle East, Iraq and Iran. He became Senior Photographer in Egypt in 1997.

Guang Niu
Born in Beijing, China, 1963

Guang moved to New York in 1995 where he started teaching himself photography. He returned to China in 1997 and took up work as a freelance photographer for Associated Press. Guang started work for Reuters in Beijing in 2000. He covers both local and regional assignments, including the SARS outbreak and the country's leadership transition.

Antony Njuguna
Born in Nairobi, Kenya, 1965

Antony started working with Reuters in 1993 as a freelance photographer based in Nairobi, East Africa and is still based there. He has covered diverse world events in the continent such as the bombing of the U.S. Embassy in Kenya, the genocide in Rwanda, wars in the Congo and Sudan, the crashing of the hijacked aeroplane in Comores and the Cricket World Cup in South Africa.

Reinhard Krause
Born in Essen, Germany, 1959

Reinhard was a staff photographer at the Essen Fair. He later worked as a freelancer for German newspapers and magazines before he joined Reuters as the Berlin Wall came down in 1989. He has been Chief Photographer for Israel and the Palestinian Territories since 2000.

Jerry Lampen
Born in Rotterdam, The Netherlands, 1961

Jerry started photography in 1981, working for local Dutch newspapers. After becoming a freelancer in 1990, Jerry started working for Reuters. He is now Reuters Chief Photographer, Netherlands. His assignments have taken him to conflict zones such as Pakistan, Israel, Palestinian Occupied Territories, Iraq and to numerous sporting events. In 2004 Jerry won first prize in the General News Single category of the World Press Photo.

Peter Macdiarmid
Born in Inverness, United Kingdom, 1964

Having worked variously in a hamburger restaurant at the BBC, in a photographic studio and once as a florist, Peter started work on *The Independent* newspaper in 1988. After a spell at *The Daily Telegraph* Peter joined Reuters as a freelancer in 2002.

Dylan Martinez
Born in Barcelona, Spain, 1969

Dylan started freelancing in London at the age of 18. At 21 he began freelancing for Reuters London and at 24 was made staff photographer based in the UK. Now based in Italy as Chief Photographer, Dylan has also covered many events in Asia and London.

Toby Melville
Born in the United Kingdom, 1970

Toby has worked as a photographer in England since 1994. He worked in the regional press before moving to the national agency Press Association in 1998. He started work for Reuters as a London-based staff photographer in 2003. His photographic awards include Nikon Photographer of the Year (2000), and Picture Editors' Guild Sports Photographer of the Year (1998).

Ethan Miller
Born in Texas, USA, 1971.

Ethan studied under Professor Frank Hoy at Arizona State University where he earned a Bachelor of Arts degree in journalism in 1994. While attending college, he worked as an intern for *The Phoenix Gazette* and *The Arizona Republic* newspapers and shot for local music magazines. Since 1995, he has been a staff photographer for the *Las Vegas Sun* newspaper and has been a

Born in Beirut, Lebanon, 1954

Ali began working for international news agencies at the beginning of the war in Lebanon in 1975. He joined Reuters in 1985 as a staff photographer, based in Lebanon initially before moving to Syria. He is currently based in Jordan as Chief Photographer.

Petr Josek

Born in Brno, former Czechoslovakia, 1952

Having worked in TV and film, Petr became a photojournalist in 1983 after participating in a news photography competition at the Czech News Agency (CTK). He joined Reuters in 1990 after the 1989 Czechoslovak Velvet revolution, and became a staff photographer in 2000.

Kamal Kishore

Born in New Delhi, India, 1966

Kamal started his career as a freelance photographer in 1985 and joined Reuters in 1987. He has covered various assignments in India, Afghanistan, Pakistan, Sri Lanka, Bhutan and has won several prizes.

Michael Kooren

Born in Curaçao, 1953

After moving to Utrecht, Holland with his parents and studying in Florida, Michael became a photographer for a student newspaper in Florida. He was a staff photographer for a regional newspaper in Utrecht for over 10 years. After freelancing for one of the largest Dutch newspapers, The *Algemeen Dagblad* for more than eight years, Michael joined Reuters in 2001.

Pawel Kopczynski

Born in Warsaw, Poland, 1971

Pawel began working as a news photographer in 1987, first for daily newspapers, then for the Polish Press Agency, and finally for Reuters, which he joined in 1995. Now based in London, he has covered a wide variety of major world events, including the war in former Yugoslavia, the Kosovo refugee crisis, the Winter Olympics, and tensions between India and Pakistan.

Viktor Korotayev

Born in Vakhtan, former USSR, 1951

Viktor became a photographer in 1974 in TASS agency. In 1989 he joined Reuters during the Perestroika period. He covered the first and second coups in Moscow, Chechen wars, Bosnia and Kosovo crises, events in Iraq and is now based in Moscow.

Born in Bobrujsk, Belarus, 1960

After school, technical university and military duty, Vasily began working in local and central Belarusian newspapers and studied photography. He started with Reuters as a freelance photographer based in the Belarus capital Minsk in 1997 and became a full-time staff photographer in 2000. He has covered events in CIS countries, Afghanistan and Liberia.

Victor Fraile

Born in Santander, Spain, 1977

Victor started work for surfing magazines, travelling through Spain, France, Indonesia, the Maldives and Hawaii. Later he worked as a freelance photographer for sports newspapers and magazines. Victor started his work as a freelancer for Reuters in 2000. He currently lives in Barcelona and works full time as a Reuters freelancer.

Eric Gaillard

Born in Nice, France, 1958

Eric began working with Agence France-Presse in 1978. He joined Reuters in 1985 when Reuters opened its news pictures service. Eric has covered Czech and Romanian revolutions, the first Gulf war, events in Israel, Bosnia, Kosovo, Iraq and Africa. Based in Nice, Eric has also covered major sporting events including the Winter and Summer Olympics and 16 Tour de France cycling races.

Tony Gentile

Born in Palermo, Italy, 1964

Tony began his career in 1989 as a photographer with a local newspaper in Sicily. He went on to work with many other national and international newspapers and magazines. In 1992 he began working as a freelance photographer for Reuters before joining the team as staff in Rome.

David Gray

Born in Sydney, Australia, 1971

David began his career with News Limited Australia, subsequently moving to Canberra Federal Parliamentary Press Gallery and *The Australian* as sports photographer. He joined Reuters in 1996 and has covered many news and sporting events throughout Asia and Australasia. Now Australia Chief Photographer, he has won several prizes including Best News Photograph in the 1999 Australian Photojournalist Awards.

Mike Hutchings

Born in London, United Kingdom, 1963

Mike began freelancing for both local and international publications in 1987 and followed the demise of Apartheid in South Africa during the turbulent 1980s. He started working for Reuters in 1991, covering the historic first democratic elections that brought Nelson Mandela to power. He has since worked across Africa and received the Abdul Sharif award at both the 1997

Born in Mannheim, Germany, 1963

Having spent some of her childhood in Ecuador, Claudia returned there in 1986 to start working as a news photographer for Editores Nacionales. In 1988 she joined Reuters as a freelancer, becoming a staff photographer in 1990 in the capital city of Quito. Currently based in Havana, Cuba, she has also worked in Santiago, Chile.

Erik de Castro
Born in Pola, Philippines, 1960

Erik started his career in photojournalism in 1980, working for a local newspaper in northern Philippines. He joined UPI three years later, before joining Reuters in 1985. Erik was named Reuters Asia's Best Photographer for 2001 for his work in Pakistan and Afghanistan after the 11 September attacks and the Muslim rebellion in southern Philippines.

Marcelo del Pozo
Born in Seville, Spain, 1970

Marcelo became a Reuters staff photographer in 2003. Based in Seville, Marcelo has covered a variety of events including the World Athletics Championships in Seville in 1999, the European Union summit in Seville in 2002, the San Fermin Bull Run in Pamplona in 2003 and the World Swimming Championships in Barcelona in 2003.

Alexander Demianchuk
Born in Kovel, Ukraine, 1959

Alexander started work for a number of Russian newspapers in 1985 before joining Reuters in 1991. Based in St Petersburg, Alexander has covered the wars in Chechnya and Iraq, as well as a range of international sporting and other events including the Summer Olympic Games in Sydney and the Salt Lake City Winter Olympics.

Kieran Doherty
Born in Dover, United Kingdom, 1968

Kieran has worked for Reuters for the whole of his career. Based in London, he has won many awards including the English Sports Council's award for Action Image of the Year and Best Sports Photo in 1998.

Bruno Domingos
Born in Rio de Janeiro, Brazil, 1977

Bruno studied physics at the Fluminense Federal University before starting his photography career in 1999 at the *Jornal Dos Sports* daily. He then worked for *Lance*, Brazil's largest sports newspaper, from 2001 to 2003. Bruno joined the Reuters bureau in Rio de Janeiro as a freelance photographer in 2003.

Born in London, United Kingdom, 1964

Desmond joined Reuters in 1992 in Madrid. He is now Chief Photographer, India based in Delhi. Desmond has covered major news, features and sport events around the world, including the Israeli-Palestinian conflict and the 2004 Iraq war.

Dani Cardona
Born in Palma de Mallorca, Spain, 1971

Dani began working as a freelance photographer for Reuters in 1997. He is based in the Balearic island of Mallorca.

Wilson Chu
Born in China, 1978

Wilson started to work as a full-time photographer at a local newspaper in 1999 following his graduation with a Bachelor degree of Law. Wilson joined Reuters Beijing in 2002.

Andy Clark
Born in Toronto, Canada, 1952

Andy has been in news photography since 1970, working for Canadian Press, Hamilton Spectator, UPI, and as the Canadian Prime Minister's photographer. Andy joined Reuters in 1987 and is now based in Vancouver, BC. He has covered many assignments including famines, disasters, world summits, sports, war in the Gulf and conflicts in the Balkans.

Claro Cortes IV
Born in Manila, Philippines, 1960

Claro started shooting as a student photographer and began contributing pictures to national publications and wire agencies before becoming a freelance photographer for UPI, which was subsequently acquired by Reuters. Based in Shanghai, China, Claro was the first recipient of the Willie Vicoy-Reuter Fellowship at the University of Missouri in Columbia in 1987.

Arko Datta
Born in Delhi, India, 1969

Arko worked for two Indian national dailies and Agence France-Presse before joining Reuters in 2001. He has covered stories in conflict regions like Iraq, Afghanistan, Kashmir, the India-Pakistan border and also the communal riots in western India and World Cup cricket. Arko has been awarded five photography prizes including Picture of the Year (Bombay Press Awards).

Yannis Behrakis
Born in Athens, Greece, 1960

Yannis began working for Reuters in 1987 and is now Chief Photographer, Greece. He has covered a variety of events including the funeral of Ayatollah Khomeini in Iran, civil conflicts in Croatia, Bosnia and Kosovo, two Gulf wars, and many international sports events. Among several prestigious awards he has been named six times News Photographer of the Year by the Greek National Fuji Awards.

Gianna Benalcázar
Born in Quito, Ecuador, 1980

Gianna is a freelance photographer and is studying design and multimedia. She focuses on social reportage.

BIOGRAPHIES

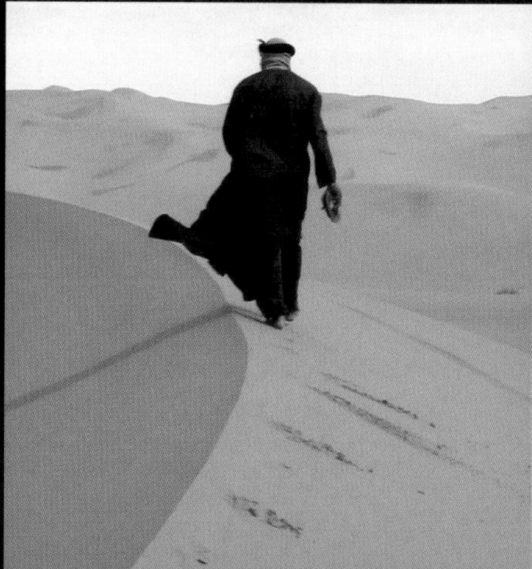

Reinhard Krause
21 April 2003

A pedestrian walks in the deserted Old City in
Jerusalem on Easter Monday.

Pawel Kopczynski

4 October 2003

Indian Army soldiers walk down the Siachen Glacier, the world's highest battlefield, which lies at the north end of the Line of Control dividing disputed Kashmir.

169

Miguel Vidal

22 February 2004

A carnival reveller dressed as a "Cigarron", an
ancient tax collector, pursues villagers through the
streets of the Spanish town of Laza hitting them
with a stick whilst ringing cowbells.

Juan Carlos Ulate

11 September 2003

An anti-WTO protester in the Mexican holiday
resort and WTO conference host city of Cancun
covers his face with a t-shirt listing the sites of
previous demonstrations.

Yannis Behrakis
20 April 2003

Iraqi Shi'ite women travel through a sandstorm to
the holy city of Kerbala for a pilgrimage previously
banned for nearly 25 years by the Saddam Hussein
regime.

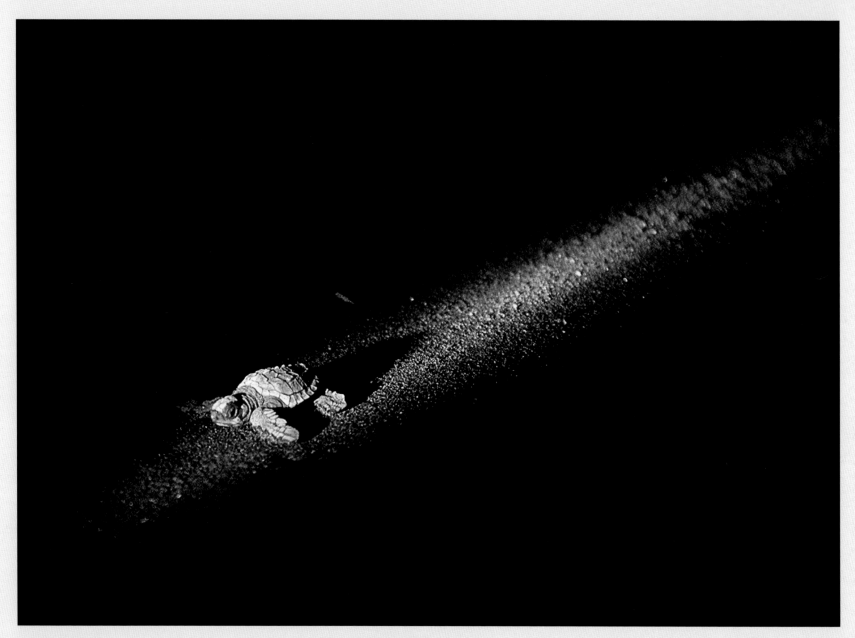

Juan Carlos Ulate

23 October 2003

A baby turtle crawls toward the sea after being
released on Ostional Beach in Santa Cruz, Costa
Rica. Only ten per cent of over five million hatched
turtles survive to become adults.

Aladin Abdel Naby
3 February 2002

A four-wheel-drive vehicle crosses sand dunes in the late afternoon sun near Egypt's western desert oasis of Siwa.

Radu Sigheti

20 December 2003

A young Kenyan Masai carries a crate of Coca-Cola
bottles to a coming-of-age ceremony in Kisaju.

Pascal Rossignol
9 December 2003

A Somali asylum seeker sips a hot drink after
sleeping outdoors in sub-freezing temperatures
near the northern French harbour of Calais, one
year after the closure of the Sangatte Red Cross
refugee camp.

Ian Waldie

11 October 2001

A British Royal Air Force C17 transport aircraft
prepares to take off from Brize Norton Royal Air
Force base in Oxfordshire.

Mike Hutchings

18 September 2002

A salvage team member climbs up to inspect a
crack in the side of a grounded Italian freighter
close to the shores of the St Lucia Wetlands Park in
South Africa.

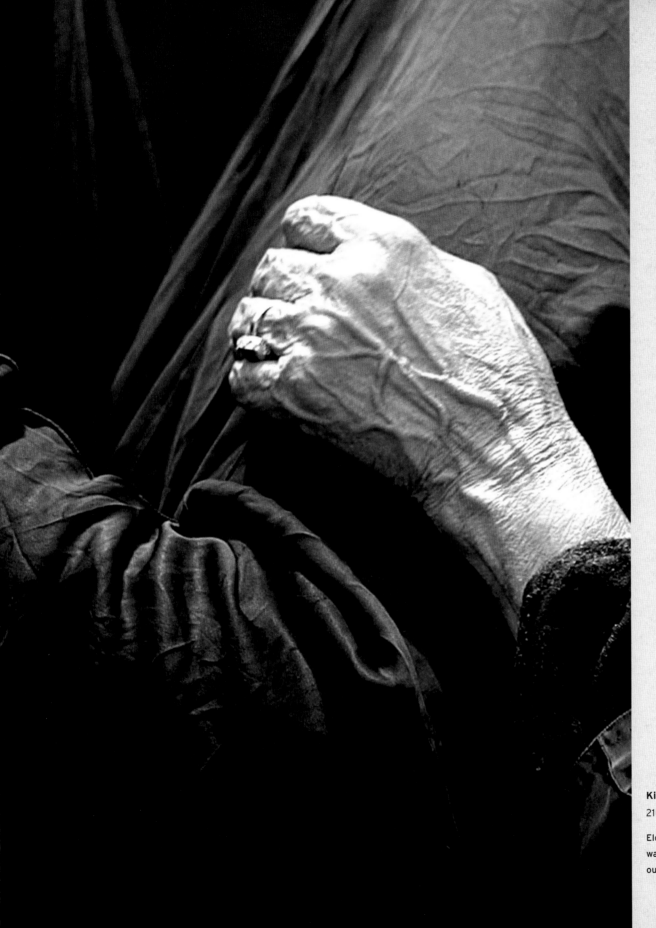

Kieran Doherty

21 May 2003

Elderly Iraqi women hold on to each other as they
wait in line for an emergency salary payment
outside the pension office in Baghdad.

157

31 December 2002

An Indian milkman carries metal pitchers of milk
during a foggy morning on the outskirts of
Amritsar, Punjab.

Paul de Bendern
14 April 2004

Kada Chouli, a guide born in the desert near the oasis town of Timimoun, walks barefoot on a sand dune in Algeria's vast Sahara desert.

31 January 2004

**A Vietnamese farmer takes pigs to a market
outside the capital Hanoi.**

Jeff J Mitchell

23 January 2003

A huskie dog team enjoys the snow ahead of the
Royal Canin Sled Dog Rally outside Aviemore in the
Highlands of Scotland.

Yannis Behrakis
24 October 2001

An Afghan man walks over a footbridge at sunset in
the northern town of Khoja Bahawuddin.

Vasily Fedosenko
1 November 2001

An Afghan man crosses the river Kokcha near the
village of Ai-Khanum in northern Afghanistan.

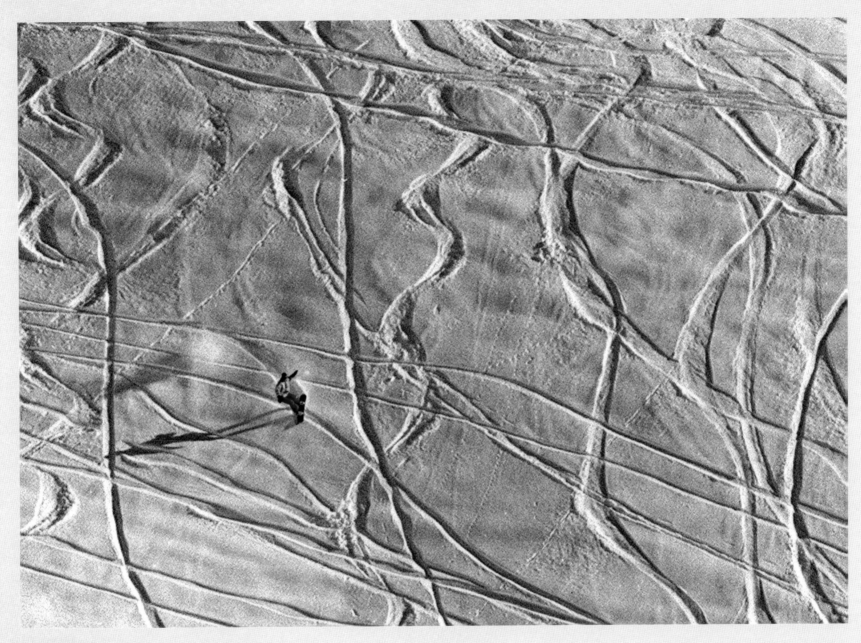

Steffen Schmidt
16 January 2000

A lone snowboarder on a mountain near the ski
resort of Arosa in Switzerland.

Jason Reed

31 May 2003

A red rose laid by U.S. First Lady Laura Bush sits between the rails of a track used to transport prisoners to the Birkenau labour and death camp where over 1.5 million prisoners lost their lives during the Second World War.

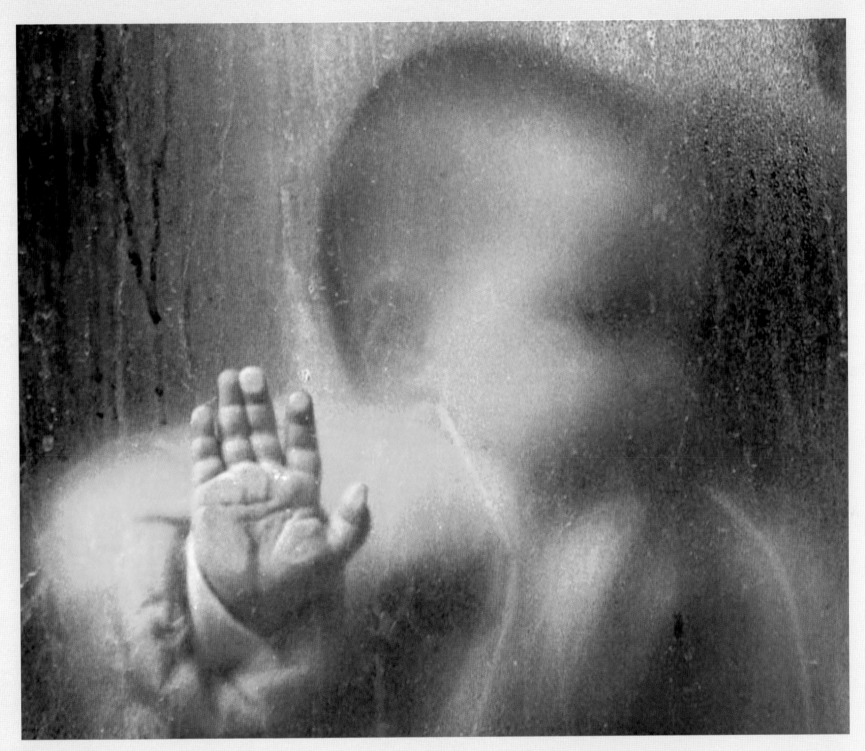

Yannis Behrakis

24 March 1999

An ethnic Albanian baby waves goodbye to her
father on a bus leaving Kosovo, bound for Turkey.

Paulo Whitaker
12 August 2003

Commuters use Sé central subway station during
rush hour in São Paulo.

Paulo Whitaker
12 August 2003

Commuters wait to board a train at Sé central
subway station in São Paulo.

Simon Kwong
22 May 2003

A traveller wearing a protective mask walks past
rows of empty luggage carts at Taipei International
Airport during the SARS epidemic.

Wilson Chu

12 October 2002

A Chinese woman arrives at a bicycle park in
Beijing to collect her bike. The majority of residents
in China's capital still use bicycles as their main
form of transportation.

Michael Kooren

22 October 2003

Cars ride around a UFO landing pad on the
outskirts of Houten. The art piece by Martin
Riebeek is intended to enable alien visitors to land
their UFOs safely in the Netherlands.

Bruno Domingos
3 August 2003

Silhouetted against a rainbow flag, two men kiss
during a protest against the Vatican's
condemnation of gay marriage, outside the Nossa
Senhora da Paz church in Rio de Janeiro.

◀ **Dimitar Dilkoff**
6 June 2002

A Bulgarian farmer herds sheep on a high altitude
meadow in the Stara Planina Mountains.

Tony Gentile
7 June 2003

Sicilian fishermen take part in the traditional
bluefin tuna mattanza in the village of Bonagia off
the western coast of Sicily.

Tim Wimborne
20 April 2004

Tourists use a chain to climb Uluru (Ayers Rock),
the world's largest monolith, although its Aboriginal
owners request that visitors respect their sacred
site and only view it from the ground.

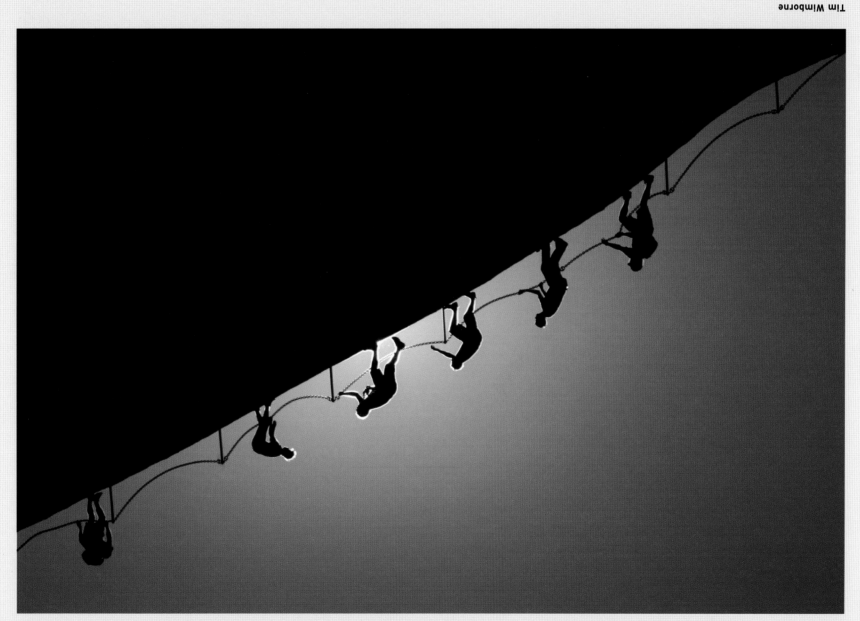

Jerry Lampen
16 December 2003

A girl peers through a gap in a plastic sheet before
the funeral of a relative in the Jabalya refugee
camp in the Gaza Strip.

Mohammed Salem
17 January 2004

A Hamas supporter holds a copy of the Koran as
she attends a demonstration in Gaza City against
plans by the French government to ban the Islamic
headscarf from schools.

Miguel Vidal
13 December 2003

Two bronze statues representing pilgrims stand on top of Monte do Gozo outside the Galician capital of Santiago de Compostela. Hundreds of thousands of pilgrims travel the long route, mostly on foot or by bicycle, many wearing the traditional sea shell badge.

Yannis Behrakis
10 April 2004

A pilgrim crawls towards the Church of the Virgin
Mary the day before Easter Sunday celebrations on
the Greek island of Tinos.

Christopher Furlong

28 September 2003

Lloyd Scott wears an antique deep sea diving suit
ahead of his 14 day 26-mile underwater marathon
below the surface of Loch Ness in Scotland, home
of the mythical monster.

Guang Niu
12 August 2003

The Great Wall of China is framed by an arch on the
outskirts of Beijing.

Mahfouz Abu Turk
7 October 2003

A Palestinian woman walks along an empty street
in the Old City of Jerusalem.

José Luis Quintana
13 October 2003

A Bolivian demonstrator jumps over a barricade in
La Paz during protests against a controversial
project to export natural gas to the United States.

Kieran Doherty

1 May 2002

A policeman in riot gear stands covered in paint in
central London during May Day demonstrations.

Stefano Rellandini
29 May 2002

The pack of riders climbs during the 163 km
sixteenth stage of the Giro d'Italia cycling race
from Conegliano to Corvara.

Kieran Doherty
5 January 2003

A stranded unmanned freighter lies beached on La
Capelle reef on the island of Guernsey.

Jeff J Mitchell

28 January 2003

A replica Viking galley is dragged through the
streets of Lerwick before a ceremonial burning
during the annual Up-Helly-Aa Festival on the island
of Shetland in Scotland.

Max Rossi
6 May 2003

New recruits of the elite Swiss Guard stand to
attention during a swearing-in ceremony at the
Vatican.

Arko Datta

24 April 2002

An Indian taxi driver walks among rows of idle taxis
during a one-day strike by drivers in Bombay.

Guang Niu
6 June 2003

A woman and her daughter ride a bicycle past an
anti-SARS banner in Beijing.

Claro Cortes IV
15 January 2004

Residents cycle along a street in China's financial
capital, Shanghai.

Andrew Wong

11 July 2001

A Chinese worker pushes a trolley past a billboard which reads "We wish Beijing success for the bid to host the Olympic Games" at Beijing International Airport.

Petr Josek
30 January 2004

A Roma resident of the North Slovakian village of Vyborna pulls a sledge with wood he collected to keep his family warm during the cold winter below the Tatra Mountains.

114

Tim Wimborne

14 May 2004

A man drives his donkey and cart along a street in
the Afghan capital Kabul.

Erik de Castro

18 February 2003

Veiled Afghan women ride in the boot of a car in
Charikar, north of Kabul.

Jerry Lampen
29 March 2003

An Iraqi girl holds her sister as she waits for her
mother to bring over food bought in Basra.

111

Shamil Zhumatov
12 February 2003

Muslim pilgrims pray after performing the symbolic
"stone the devil" ritual in Mena, during the last
stage of the Haj pilgrimage.

Akram Saleh

27 June 2003

Iraqis walk down the steps of the famous Samarra
mosque minaret.

Yannis Behrakis

31 March 2004

Gianna Angelopoulos, president of the Athens 2004
organizing committee, holds a torch with the
Olympic Flame in the Panathenaic Stadium, where
the first modern Olympics took place in 1896.

Bruno Domingos
22 February 2004

Revellers parade atop the float of the Unidos da
Tijuca Samba School during a competition at the
Sambodrome in Rio de Janeiro.

Bruno Domingos
29 June 2003

A man dressed in drag during the Gay Pride parade
in Rio de Janeiro.

Alexander Demianchuk

11 February 2004

Seen through ice patterns on glass, a pedestrian
braving temperatures of -20°C walks along
Dvortsovaya Embankment in St Petersburg.

Alexander Demianchuk
2 October 2003

The Church of the Spilt Blood and a silhouette of a
walking woman are reflected in a puddle in
St Petersburg, Russia.

Andy Clark
18 October 2002

A jogger takes a break while running on the seawall
in Stanley Park as downtown Vancouver is
enveloped by an early morning mist.

Yannis Behrakis
5 July 2004

Hundreds of thousands of Greek fans welcome the
triumphant national soccer team from the Euro
2004 championship to the Panathenaic Stadium in
Athens.

Peter Macdiarmid

15 February 2003

Anti-war protesters gather in London at the start of
a demonstration against war on Iraq. Millions of
people took to the streets of towns and cities
across the globe to demonstrate against the
looming U.S.-led war on Iraq.

Viktor Korotayev

2 July 2004

A small plane flies at sunset near the village of
Tyazhino, 50 km southeast of Moscow.

Tony Gentile

1 March 2003

A masked woman dressed in traditional carnival costume takes part in celebrations at St Mark's Square in Venice.

95

Dani Cardona

27 August 2003

Revellers fight in tomato pulp during the annual
"Tomatina" battle in Bunyol, Spain.

Kieran Doherty

21 June 2003

Revellers watch a bubble as it floats into the air at
sunrise on the day of the summer solstice at
Stonehenge in southern England.

Victor Fraile

14 October 2002

A surfer carries his board as the sun sets during
the international surfing competition in Mundaka,
northern Spain.

Yannis Behrakis

13 June 2001

A schoolgirl jumps on a trampoline as a tourist
slides on a "flying fox" wire into the sea at an
Athens beach.

Kamal Kishore
11 August 2002

Vegetable sellers trade at a floating market on Dal
Lake in Srinagar, the summer capital of Jammu and
Kashmir.

Utpal Baruah
29 July 2004

An Indian girl rows a raft made from banana tree
shoots in Samata, northeastern India, following the
worst floods in years.

Andrew Wong

23 May 2004

A Chinese sailor rests on the banks of the Mekong
River as he waits for his Thailand-bound cargo
vessel to be loaded at the Guanlei port in the
southwestern province of Yunnan.

Wilson Chu

30 June 2004

A Chinese tourist rests against an outer wall of
Beijing's 600-year-old Forbidden City.

Claudia Daut
14 June 2003

Thousands of Cubans rally to honour the late
guerrilla leader Ernesto "Che" Guevara in Santa
Clara where he led the main battle for the Cuban
revolution in 1959.

Claro Cortes IV

18 July 2002

A Chinese woman struggles to cross a busy
intersection in Shanghai.

Peter Morgan

5 December 2002

A street performer known as the "Naked Cowboy" sings in Times Square in New York as a snowstorm hits the city. He said he was not cold because he was "burning with desire".

Stefano Rellandini

14 November 2001

A man walks in the middle of St Mark's Square
flooded by high water in Venice.

China Photo
11 February 2003

Chinese migrant workers are reflected on the glass wall of a crowded train station during snow fall in Wuhan.

Paulo Whitaker
27 February 2003

A vendor walks past a wall decorated with figures of Baianas, the theme of the Carnival in Salvador, northern Brazil.

Kamal Kishore
13 July 2004

Flood-affected villagers ride a boat to reach safety
in Mandakata, northeast India.

Petr Josek
11 July 1997

A dog tries to find a dry place through flood water along a street in the town of Uherske Hradiste in the Czech southern Moravian city.

Peter Macdiarmid

31 October 2003

Paul Hardwick, second "whipper in" at the Beaufort Hunt Kennels prepares to allow foxhounds out to exercise in Badminton in the southern English county of Gloucestershire.

74

Antony Njuguna
24 September 2003

A Somali truck loaded with corn is parked on the
side of a road in Mogadishu.

73

Toby Melville

13 April 2003

The shadow of Britain's Paula Radcliffe (left) is
seen flanked by her pacemaker Samson Lopuyet
(right) on her way to winning the women's 26th
London Marathon.

Paul Vreeker

15 December 2003

Members of the Dutch Royal Guard guide their
horses through clouds of thick smoke and gunfire
on the beach of Scheveningen near The Hague.

Gianna Benalcázar
9 April 2004

An Ecuadorean penitent with chains on his feet
participates in a Good Friday procession in Quito.

Bazuki Muhammad

19 January 2003

A Hindu devotee performs "anga pradesha", a ritual
where he rolls his body for 2 km as a form of
penance, on his procession to the Batu Caves
Temple, during the Thaipusam festival in Kuala
Lumpur.

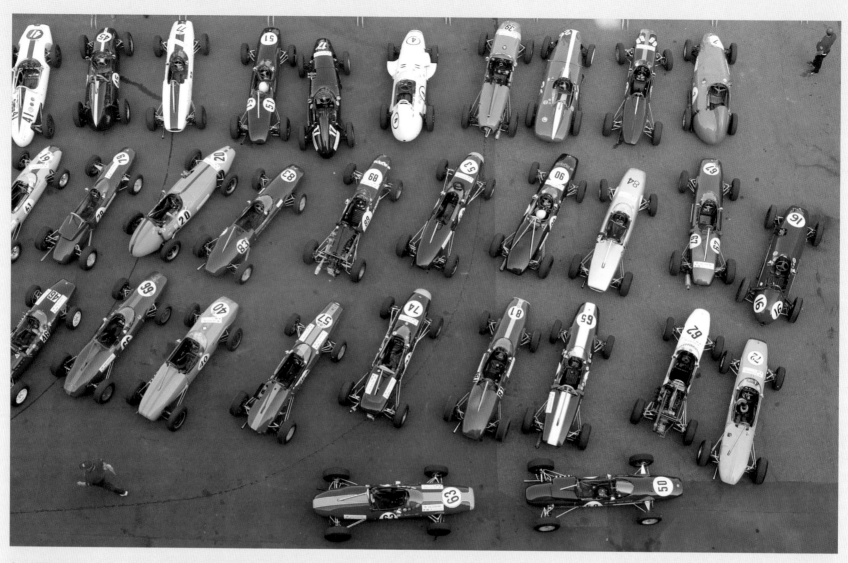

Arnd Wiegmann

6 August 2004

A man walks past former Formula Junior race cars
during the AvD-Oldtimer-Grand Prix at the west
German Nürburgring circuit.

Ethan Miller
17 July 2004

Cars travel on State Route 157 as a thunderstorm
flashes in the distance in the Mount Charleston
area of the Spring Mountains range, Nevada.

Arko Datta

21 June 2003

An Afghan man looks at picture postcards of
popular Bollywood stars in Kabul.

Radu Sigheti

28 January 2003

A member of Noknesset fixes stickers of his
organization over banners of different Israeli
parties in Yitzhak Rabin Square in Tel Aviv during
parliamentary elections. Noknesset favours the
abolition of the Israeli parliament.

Thomas White

17 March 2004

Commuters board a subway train at Taipei's main
station. Announcements on Taipei's subway trains
are made in three Chinese dialects.

Fabrizio Bensch

12 November 2003

Seated German anti-nuclear protesters take cover
under plastic sheets on a road in the small village
of Grippel, as they block the transportation of
nuclear waste containers.

Pawel Kopczynski
29 April 2004

Polish riot police watch as anti-globalization
demonstrators march through Warsaw during a
European economic summit.

Bobby Yip

20 March 2000

A Buddhist nun holding a Taiwanese flag confronts
riot police outside the Nationalist Party
headquarters in Taipei.

Guang Niu
2 July 2004

Young Mongolian monks hide behind the door of the
Amarbayasgalan Monastery in Erdene, around
500 km northwest of the capital Ulan Bator.

Shannon Stapleton
28 August 2003

A man going by the name "Shaman Cat" watches
the sunset at the annual Burning Man Festival in
the Nevada Desert.

Desmond Boylan
16 January 2003

A rider and his horse pass through a bonfire during the annual Saint Anthony purification ceremony in the Spanish village of San Bartolome de los Pinares.

Ali Jarekji
8 March 2004

A Palestinian refugee wearing a prayer dress looks
out from her home at the al-Hussein refugee camp
in Amman, Jordan.

55

Jorge Silva

29 March 2002

An elderly Guatemalan Catholic penitent takes part
in the solemn procession of "Senor Sepultado"
during Good Friday celebrations through the
colonial city of Antigua.

Damir Sagolj

25 June 2004

Religious statues are on sale to pilgrims on the site where the Virgin Mary reportedly appeared to six Bosnian youngsters in Medjugorje. Millions of pilgrims from all over the world visit the small Bosnian town each year.

Miguel Vidal

6 April 2004

Hooded penitents wait for the start of the 'Santisimo
Cristo de la Paciencia' brotherhood procession in
Santiago de Compostela, northern Spain.

51

Dylan Martinez

22 February 2004

Venetians dressed in traditional costumes stroll
through St Mark's Square as the sun sets on the
Venice Carnival.

Eliana Aponte

22 February 2004

Members of the Brazilian Salgueiro Samba School
dance at the Sambodrome in Rio de Janeiro.

Jim Hollander

6 July 2000

A reveller attending the Spanish Fiesta de San Fermin leaps off a statue into the waiting arms of friends as the week-long festival gets under way in Pamplona.

Paolo Cocco
1 October 2002

People walk in front of Rome's ancient Colosseum
lit with bright gold lights.

Alessandro Bianchi

18 April 2004

A man dressed as a Roman centurion marches in
front of a marble map depicting the old Roman
empire during a parade in Rome.

Miguel Vidal
6 July 2003

Hundreds of wild horses are rounded up, trimmed
and groomed during the "Rapa Das Bestas" event
in Sabucedo, Spain.

David Gray

26 September 2002

Graham Finlayson herds some of his remaining
sheep on his drought-ridden property in remote
New South Wales, Australia.

Remy Steinegger
9 March 2003

11,262 cross-country skiers race over the frozen
Lake Sils during the 42 km Engadine Ski Marathon
in Switzerland.

Radu Sigheti
4 August 2004

A Sudanese refugee rides his donkey at dusk as he
crosses a dry riverbed near a refugee camp in
eastern Chad.

Andy Clark

17 June 2004

A passenger stands on the deck of the Queen of
Coquitlam ferry during a crossing from Vancouver
Island to the Canadian mainland.

Darren Whiteside
15 August 1998

Cambodian men, riding between rail carriages to avoid paying the fare, make their way to the southern port of Kampot.

Arko Datta

16 January 2003

A boy looks through a window of a Japanese
"Peace Boat" during a function held by Indian and
Japanese peace activists to mark the inaugural day
of the World Social Forum in Bombay.

Suhaib Salem

16 February 2003

Iraqi soldiers march through the courtyard of the
Martyrs' Monument in Baghdad.

Damir Sagolj

28 October 2003

U.S. Army soldiers ride a confiscated motorcycle in the nothern Iraqi town of Tikrit. Motorcycles were forbidden by occupation forces after being used in attacks on U.S. troops.

Mahfouz Abu Turk
5 January 2004

A Palestinian boy runs in front of the controversial
security barrier on the outskirts of Jerusalem.

Natalie Behring

19 December 2001

An Armenian Orthodox priest walks through the
nave of the Church of the Nativity, believed to be
the birth place of Jesus Christ, in the West Bank
town of Bethlehem.

Andrew Wong
27 September 2002

An elderly Chinese woman has her hair cut on a
pavement in Beijing.

Erik Gaillard

14 July 2002

An old man watches the pack of riders make its way
past his house in the village of Landujan in Brittany
during the eighth stage of the 89th Tour de France.

David Gray

4 December 2003

Fasten your seatbelts. An airliner flies towards
storm clouds after taking off from Sydney Airport.

Tim Wimborne

2 February 2004

The Ghan outback train heads north in Australia's
Northern Territory. The 1 km-long train runs
2,979 km from Adelaide to Darwin and is named
after Afghan camel drivers who used their animals to
carry goods over a similar route over 150 years ago.

Dylan Martinez

19 May 2000

A woman peers out from the back of a taxi at a
roadblock set up by British peacekeeping soldiers
on the outskirts of Freetown, Sierra Leone.

Damir Sagolj
23 November 2001

Afghan refugees ride on a truck with their
belongings as they pass through Maidan Shahr on
their way back home to Kabul.

Rafiqur Rahman

29 December 2003

An overcrowded train leaves a platform in Tongi
near Bangladesh's capital Dhaka, as two million
pilgrims attend the final day of the annual Biswa
Ijtema, the world's second biggest Muslim
gathering after the Haj.

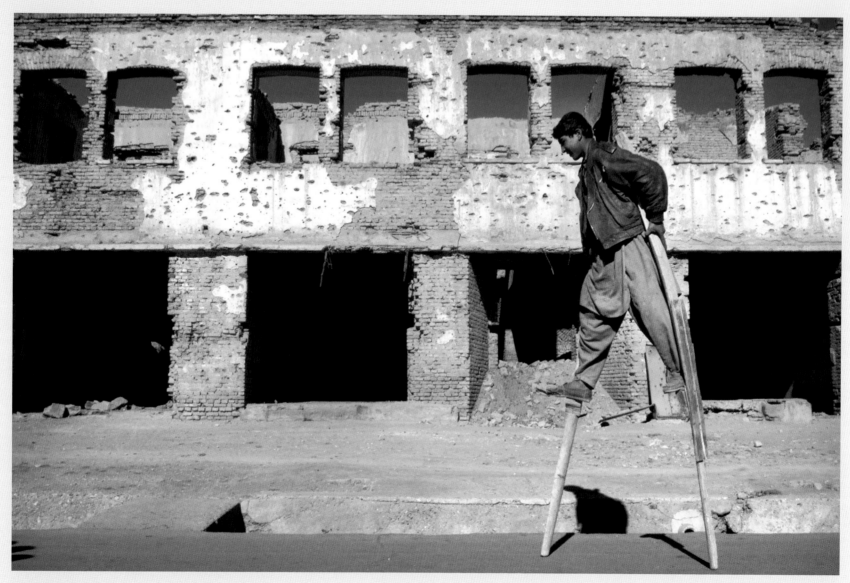

Damir Sagolj

4 December 2001

Karim, a 16-year-old Afghan boy, walks on stilts in a
war-shattered suburb of Kabul.

Vincent West
8 July 2004

A child pushes a toy bull as he runs through central
Pamplona during the Spanish Fiesta de San Fermin.

Max Rossi

23 July 2003

Performers take to the cobbled streets of the central Italian town of Certaldo during a traditional festival to promote the ancient art of circus entertainment.

Damir Sagolj

13 July 2004

Fighting bulls approach a barrier during the
seventh bull run of the Spanish Fiesta de San
Fermin in Pamplona. A pack of six fighting bulls and
steers runs through the town centre to the bullring
every morning during the week-long festival.

Marcelo del Pozo

12 July 2003

A boy is showered in sparks from the "Fire Bull", a man with a metal figure of a bull loaded with fireworks at the Spanish Fiesta de San Fermin in Pamplona.

Arko Datta
10 June 2003

An Afghan boy takes water home in buckets. Without
access to drinking water in their homes, many Kabul
residents are forced to travel miles in order to
source water from wells and public outlets.

Carlos Barria

14 October 2003

Bolivians walk on the deserted streets of El Alto
following a day of violence during the fourth week
of anti-government protests.

Bobby Yip
1 July 2004

Pro-democracy protestors march on a main street
in Hong Kong on the seventh anniversary of the
territory's handover to China.